THE SATURDAY ADVENTURE

Sally Prue
Illustrated by Shoo Rayner

Chapter 1

Mum worked on Saturdays, so Ellie and Louis always spent the day with Dad. They had many adventures.

One Friday evening, there was some bad news.

"Jessica is coming to stay," said Dad.

Ellie and Louis groaned and groaned. Jessica was their cousin and she was no fun at all. She wore silly frilly socks and she was always so clean and perfect.

The next day, Jessica arrived in a clean white dress and shiny black shoes.

"Look at my lovely new watch," she boasted. "It's much nicer than anything you've got, isn't it?"

Louis and Ellie looked at Jessica. How could you have adventures in a clean white dress, shiny black shoes and a brand new watch?

“Let’s go to the park,” said Dad brightly.

“Oh, no,” said Louis. “Not the park.”

“The park’s for little kids,” said Ellie. “You can’t have adventures in the park.”

“Well, I’d like to go to the park,” said Jessica.

So they went to the park.

“What would you like to play on, Jessica?” asked Dad.

“I’d like to go on the swings,” said Jessica. “You can come and push me, and Ellie and Louis can look after my new watch.”

Ellie and Louis put Jessica's watch on the park bench. Then they sat and waited while Dad pushed Jessica on the swings.

"This is boring," said Louis. "I'd rather play pirates."

"So would I," said Ellie, "and I know who I'd make to walk the plank!"

Ellie and Louis watched Jessica on the swing. She swung backwards and forwards, backwards and forwards.

And backwards.

And forwards.

"I'm going to die of boredom if something exciting doesn't happen soon," said Ellie.

Louis was so bored he decided to do a handstand.

"Be careful you don't knock the watch," said Ellie.

"Where is it?" asked Louis.

"It's on the bench," said Ellie.

But Jessica's new watch was nowhere to be seen.

"Oh, no!" gasped Ellie. "Where is it?"

They looked for the watch everywhere.

It wasn't on the bench.

It wasn't on the ground.

It wasn't anywhere.

"Jessica will be finished on the swings soon," said Louis. "What are we going to do?"

"There's only one thing we can do," said Ellie. "RUN!"

Chapter 2

Ellie and Louis ran down to the edge of the lake.

"Where shall we go?" asked Louis.

"Let's escape on a boat," said Ellie. "It's our only hope."

"Pedal faster!" said Ellie. "Left! Right! Left! Right!"

The boat moved out steadily across the lake. In the middle of the lake there was a tiny island covered with trees.

“We could hide on that island,” said Louis.

“We’ll have to hide much further away than that,” said Ellie. “Let’s see what’s on the other side of the lake.”

When they got to the other side of the lake they saw big houses with high walls and signs that said "Private" and "Keep out!" Behind the walls there was a huge dog that looked like it might bite.

“Looks like we’ll have to hide on the island after all,” said Ellie.

“What will we eat?” asked Louis.

“Fish,” said Ellie.

“I don’t like fish,” said Louis.

"Maybe there will be some fruit trees on the island," said Ellie. "You like fruit."

Ellie and Louis hopped out of the boat and tugged at it. It was heavy.

"Oh, leave the boat there," said Ellie. "It will be fine."

As they were looking for some food, Ellie and Louis heard a rustling sound.

"What was that?" Louis asked.

The rustling sound got louder.

"Maybe it's a lion," whispered Ellie.

"Maybe it's a bear," cried Louis.

"Maybe it's . . . a snake!" they both screamed.

"Quick!" said Ellie. "Into that tree!"

"We can't stay here forever," said Louis.

Ellie sighed. "We'll have to go back to the boat," she decided.

Then Louis pointed a trembling finger. The boat was floating away out on the lake.

"Oh, no!" cried Louis. "What are we going to do now? We're stuck here."

"Give me your shirt," said Ellie.

"What?" asked Louis.

"Trust me," said Ellie. "I have a plan."

Ellie climbed higher up the tree. She climbed up past a bird's nest and a big, black crow cawed at her angrily.

Ellie got to the top of the tree and waved Louis' shirt as high as she could.

But nobody noticed her.

Ellie began to climb down. The crow's nest had three eggs in it.

"No wonder the crow was angry with me," she thought.

Then she saw something shiny in the nest . . .

"*Jessica's watch*!" Ellie shouted.

Jessica's watch sparkled in the sun, and that gave Ellie an idea about how to show Dad where they were. She held the watch so that the sunlight bounced right into Dad's face.

That made him notice her!

"It was very brave to chase after the crow to get Jessica's watch back," said Dad. "But you should have asked for my help."

"But we didn't need help," said Ellie.

"No," said Dad, "but I missed the adventure!"

“And so did I,” cried Jessica, stamping her foot.

“What?” Ellie, Louis and Dad all said together.

“It’s not fair,” Jessica pouted. “Every other kid I know has fun, while I have to wear these silly frilly clothes and stay clean. I want to have adventures, too!”

Ellie and Louis looked at each other.

"You could borrow some of my clothes to play in," said Ellie.

"And then we could all have adventures," said Louis. "Lots of adventures!"